All the Little Animals

A Bedtime Book from A-Z

JOY JORDAN-LAKE

ILLUSTRATIONS BY JANE CHAPMAN

An Imprint of Thomas Nelson

All the Little Animals

© 2024 Joy Jordan-Lake

Tommy Nelson, PO Box 141000, Nashville, TN 37214

Published in Nashville, Tennessee, by Tommy Nelson. Tommy Nelson is an imprint of Thomas Nelson. Thomas Nelson is a registered trademark of HarperCollins Christian Publishing, Inc.

Tommy Nelson titles may be purchased in bulk for educational, business, fund-raising, or sales promotional use. For information, please email SpecialMarkets@ThomasNelson.com.

ISBN 978-1-4002-4844-5 (eBook)
ISBN 978-1-4002-4852-0 (HC)

Library of Congress Cataloging-in-Publication Data

Names: Jordan-Lake, Joy, 1963- author. | Chapman, Jane, 1970- illustrator.
Title: All the little animals : a bedtime book from A-Z / Joy Jordan-Lake ;
   illustrations by Jane Chapman.
Description: Nashville, Tennessee : Thomas Nelson, 2024. | Audience: Ages
   4-8. | Summary: From aardvarks to zebras and everyone in between, baby
   zoo animals go through their bedtime routines as they snuggle up, say
   good night, and drift off to dream.
Identifiers: LCCN 2023040727 (print) | LCCN 2023040728 (ebook) | ISBN
   9781400248520 (hardcover) | ISBN 9781400248445 (epub)
Subjects: CYAC: Stories in rhyme. | Bedtime--Fiction. | Alphabet--Fiction.
   | Zoo animals--Fiction. | LCGFT: Stories in rhyme. | Picture books.
Classification: LCC PZ8.3.J7714 Al 2024 (print) | LCC PZ8.3.J7714 (ebook)
   | DDC [E]--dc23
LC record available at https://lccn.loc.gov/2023040727
LC ebook record available at https://lccn.loc.gov/2023040728

Printed in Malaysia

24 25 26 27 28 COS 10 9 8 7 6 5 4 3 2 1

Mfr: COS / Johor, Malaysia / April 2024 / PO #12240163

For my precious older daughter, Julia, who made bedtime
a beautiful adventure of books and songs.

For my great-grandmother Anne Elizabeth Hopson Wood,
who inspired this book with her nighttime ritual for children.

And for all the Jordan, Jordan-Lake, Jackson-Jordan, and Owen
descendants who've drifted off to sleep with all the little animals.

—Joy

For my own little babies, who grew up to be bigger than me.

—Jane

All the little animals under the sun,
in the **wild**, and in every zoo

are yawning and nuzzling and snuggling and huddling, getting ready for sleep, **just like you**.

All the little **Armadillos** line up each night
to sleep in their dens underground,

while baby **Bats** clamp their claws into place
to doze in a cave upside down.

All the little **Cassowaries** crowd into nests
as their daddies smooth down each feather,

while wee golden **Dingoes** quit prowling the deserts and pack in to nuzzle together.

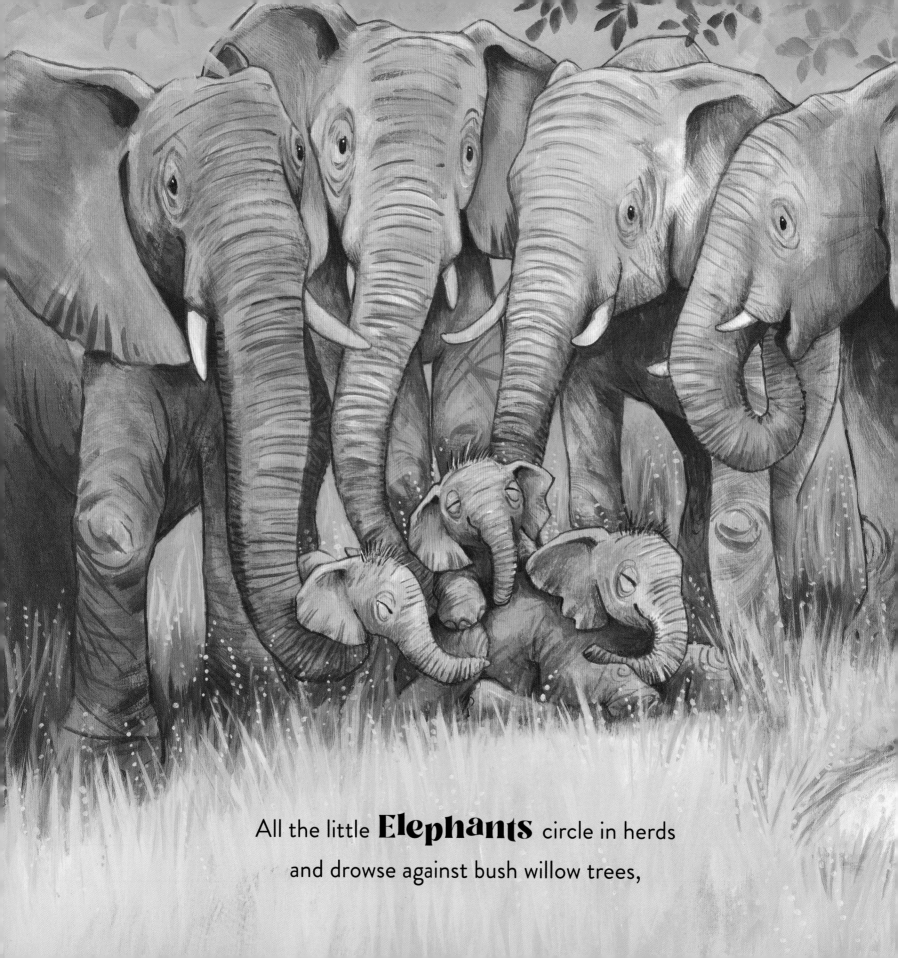

All the little **Elephants** circle in herds
and drowse against bush willow trees,

while young **Flamingos**
tuck in under Mom,
who can sleep while she's locking her knees.

The little **Giraffes** all rest weary heads
on top of their small spotted rumps,

while round baby **Hippos** snooze in the river,
just nostrils on top of brown bumps.

All the little **Ibis**, circled by sticks,

sleep well, not a chirp or a flap,

while each of the **Jaguars**

lets out a big yawn

when it's time to curl up for catnaps.

The little **Koalas** all cuddle for hours and snuggle in Mom's comfy pouch,

while sleek, teensy **Lizards**

each fold in their frills

and cling to a branch in a crouch.

All the little **Moose** calves
nap in the woods
and doze lying down in the snow,

while undersized **Newts**
love to loll under logs
and laze in the cool mud below.

All the little **Orcas**
get towed behind Mom,
with the currents and waves
keeping beat,

while emperor **Penguins**
huddle so close,
all folded in warmth at Dad's feet.

All the little **Quokkas**
slip into Mom's sack
as they drowse and their eyes
start to close,

while soft baby **Rabbits**

hop so hard they collapse

when, at last, they nod off

nose-to-nose.

All the little **Sea otters** hold hands as they float
and let seaweed twine them in tight,

while small marine **Turtles** fold front flippers up
and dream sweet turtle dreams through the night.

All the little **Unaus** move oh-so slo-o-owly,
feet hooked on a branch as they sleep,

while small, fuzzy **Vultures** in nests hidden well
nod off as they nestle in deep.

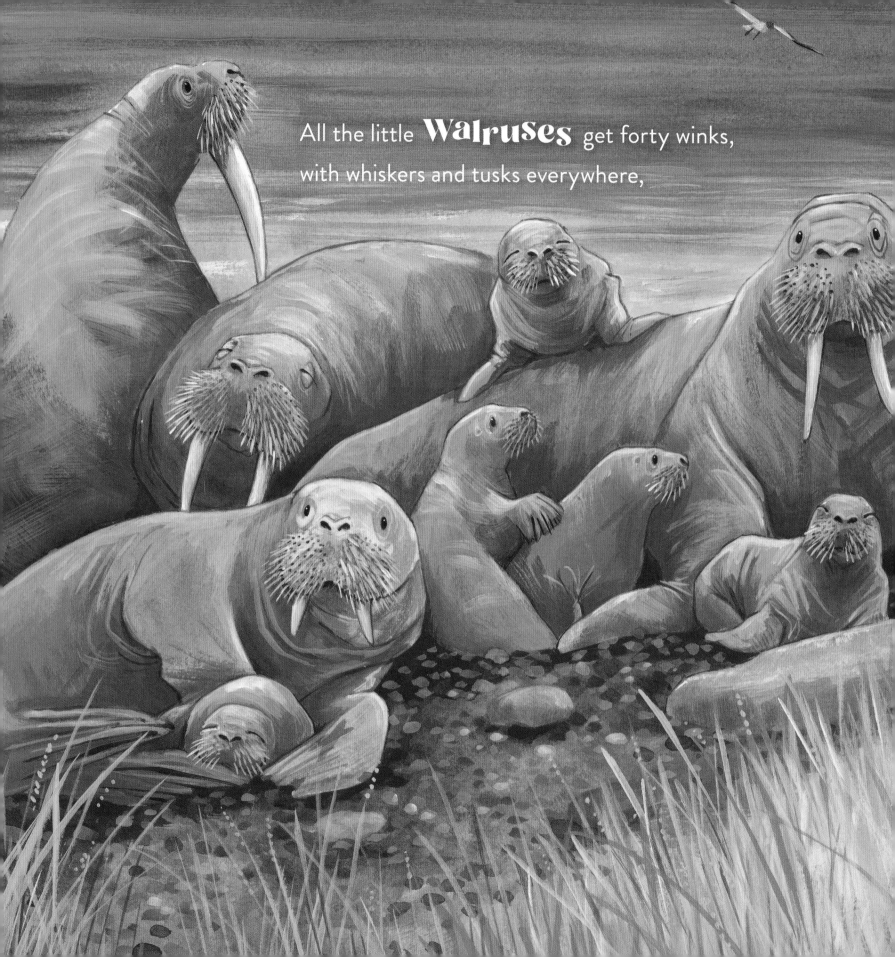

All the little **Walruses** get forty winks,
with whiskers and tusks everywhere,

while tiny **Xemes** dream of stretching their wings
as they glide through the cold arctic air.

All the little **Yaks**

nap in mountainous lands

as they press close to Mom's shaggy coat,

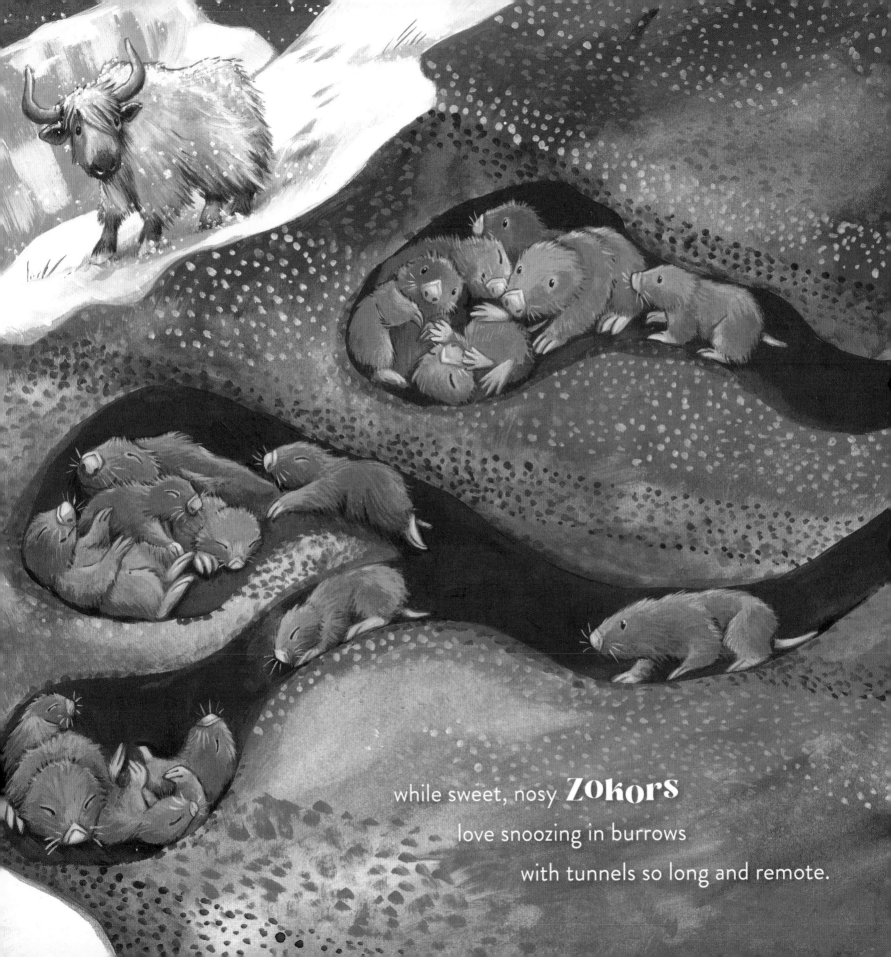

while sweet, nosy **Zokors**

love snoozing in burrows

with tunnels so long and remote.

So just like the animals going to sleep,

now it's your turn to squeeze your eyes tight.

Curl up, sweet one, and know you're so loved.

It's time for a hug and **good night**.